A TREASURE TROVE OF TIMELESS TALES

Shobha Tharoor Srinivasan is an award-winning voice-over artist, poet, editor, and author of a dozen works of fiction and nonfiction. She is also a former non-profit development professional who spent two decades as an advocate and fundraiser for persons with disabilities. She won the 68th National Film Awards for Best Narration Voiceover for the film *Rhapsody of Rains-Monsoons of Kerala,* in 2022.

Shobha has published children's books in India and the United States, including the award-winning *Indi-Alphabet* (Mango and Marigold), *Prince with a Paintbrush: The Story of Raja Ravi Varma* (Westland), *It's Time to Rhyme* (Aleph), and *Parvati the Elephant's Very Important Day* (Harper Collins). Her first book for adults, *Good Innings* (Penguin), is being translated into Malayalam.

Shobha's love of words and stories began in childhood with storytelling sessions and word play with her siblings. When she is not travelling in search of stories, Shobha lives in Campbell, California, with her husband. When she's not writing, doing voice-overs or multi-tasking, she can be found playing fun-grandmom to her two grandchildren, reading books or telling tales from around the world.

A Treasure Trove of TIMELESS TALES

Shobha Tharoor Srinivasan

Illustrations by

Mistunee

Published by Red Panda, an imprint of Westland Books, a division of Nasadiya Technologies Private Limited, in 2022

No. 269 I 2B, First Floor, 'Irai Arul', Vimalraj Street, Nethaji Nagar, Allappakkam Main Road, Maduravoyal, Chennai 600095

Westland, the Westland logo, Red Panda and the Red Panda logo are the trademarks of Nasadiya Technologies Private Limited, or its affiliates.

A version of the stories, 'The Sun, the Wind, the Moon and the Sky', 'The Doll in a Red Sari' and 'The Lovable Thief' first appeared in *A Pie Surprise and Other Stories* (Mango Books).

ISBN: 9789395073646

10 9 8 7 6 5 4 3

Typeset by New Media Line Creations

Printed at Manipal Technologies Limited, Manipal

For Mrinalini and Shai, who inspire my stories with their abundant curiosity and imagination.

CONTENTS

Author's Note

What you hold in your hands or electronic device is not just a book. It is a vault—a treasure trove—of stories written and put together with great care to ensure that you enjoy both the diversity in the themes presented, and the distinct styles of narration in each. The common thread unifying the stories is that they are all rooted in the past—my past, your past, our past. These are memories from my childhood, retellings of folk tales and parables that have been handed down for generations, and narratives prompted by recent recollections. Each story offers lessons to be learnt, but they are written without preachy or didactic tones.

A Treasure Trove of Timeless Tales includes tales from around the world, from Japanese folklore to the Puranas. I have retold a Native American folk tale, shared a tribal tale inspired by oral storytelling traditions, and written stories in which animals do the talking. Together, they speak the message of '*one world, many stories*' and '*one story, many worlds*'.

The stories have been composed using different narrative styles. *The Doll in a Red Sari* is written in the first person, while the retelling of classical Jataka tales, Panchatantra stories and Aesop's Fables has been done using a modern conversational style. *Kayamkullam Kochunni* is a historical narrative, and the *Lockdown Stories* are short, 100-word imaginative tales that encourage readers to create their own.

I am excited to share these stories with you, dear reader. I hope that you find resonance in these narratives and enjoy discovering in these stories others who have overcome obstacles, been on adventures, and made a difference in the world, just as you have.

So much about writing and reading is about discovery for both the author and the reader. When one teaches, two learn. Play with words. Read more stories. And please do share with others.

Shobha Tharoor Srinivasan
Campbell, California

The Sun, the Wind, the Moon and the Sky

There are many variations of this folk tale, retold in India, even today. I heard it as a child, narrated it to my offspring, and now share its creative teaching moments with my grandchildren. The story of the Sun, the Wind, the Moon and the Sky draws attention to the qualities of selflessness, generosity and compassion by pointing out the pitfalls of pride, selfishness and self-importance.

'Just one more story, please, Amma,' Renuka pleaded as she climbed into bed.

'Ok kanna, a last one,' her mother replied with a smile.

She tucked the blankets around Renuka's shoulders to keep the child in bed and not clamour for more after the story. The eight-year-old grinned impishly, pleased about the extra time before Amma switched the lights off. She waited for her favourite story—the tale of the sun, the wind, the moon and the sky.

'Long, long ago, when the world was still young, the Sun, the Wind and the Moon went to feast with their uncle and aunt, Thunder and Lightning. Their mother, the Sky, whose many duties prevented her from accompanying them for such outings, wished them a happy time. She continued to hold up the world and awaited their return.

Both the Sun and the Wind were thoughtless, selfish boys. They forgot about their mother as soon as they left her. On the other hand, Moon, who trailed behind, kept thinking about their mother, who couldn't join them.

When the boys reached their uncle and aunt's house, they were not disappointed. Long tables were laden with fruits and vegetables. There were large fleshy jackfruits piled on glittering plates, juicy mangoes and papayas heaped into sparkling bowls, and jewelled yams and colourful peppers laid out on silver trays. There were savoury offerings as well.

After getting the greetings out of the way, Sun and Wind rushed to the tables and gorged on mounds of fragrant biryani smothered with raisins and cashew nuts. They stuffed themselves with long green okra fried to perfection. And filled their mouths with soft fish marinated in ginger, tomatoes and chilli powder. They ate until they thought they would burst and thought only of themselves.

On the other hand, their sister, the gentle Moon, ate only a little of the feast offered. She thought of her mother whose responsibilities had kept her away from the feast. She saved a portion of her food to take home. Moon did not have the strength and power her brothers did, but she was kind and thoughtful and loved to share and give.

'Children, how was the feast,' Sky asked Sun, Wind and Moon on their return.

'Did you bring anything back for me?' She merely posed the question to test them. She was more interested in their response than any gift or food offering.

'What do you mean, Mother?' Sun asked insolently. 'Why should we bring anything for you? We did not go for such a purpose. We were invited as guests for dinner. Besides, you are not used to the rich food and delicacies we ate. You would not have enjoyed the feast.'

Wind blustered as well and followed his bold brother's lead. 'How could we have carried the food with us, Mother? We went out in fine robes. Our pockets would have become dirty, and the food would have soiled our elegant clothes. You cannot expect that of us!'

Sky then turned to her daughter, Moon. Noticing her mother's disappointed face, Moon said, 'I have brought you samples of all the food we ate, dear Mother. You should have your dinner now.'

'May you live long, my child,' Sky said with pride. Turning to her sons, she exclaimed, 'You will lose much due to your selfishness, boys. You, my eldest, went out to feast and never thought of your mother, although she supports you all day and is your protector. You shall always live in an eternal fire. Your rays will be scorching and shall burn all that it touches. Men and women will stay away from you when you blaze in pride.'

Turning to Wind, she said, 'And you, greedy Wind, will always blow in dry weather and parch and shrivel those you touch. Men and women will be inconvenienced and take shelter away from you when you are around.'

She looked at Moon with pride. 'But you, my sweet daughter, who thought more of another than yourself, will endure always. You shall be cool, calm and beautiful. Your soft hue will inspire poetry and song. Men, women and children with marvel at your beauty and charm. They will be full of love when they see you. You will always be blessed and cherished.'

'That is why the Sun is disliked when it beats down too hotly, isn't it Amma?' asked Renuka.

'Yes, and the Wind is disliked when it blows too strongly,' replied her mother.

'And the Moon is loved by all,' Renuka smiled dreamily as her eyes began to grow heavy.

She kissed her mother and settled in to sleep with her head full of plans for the next day. 'Tomorrow, I will make my bed as soon as I wake up. I will tidy the toys and books on my bedroom floor, so no one steps on them. Tomorrow I will help Appa clear up the leaves in the garden. I am going to be a good helper from now on. I am going to share more ...'

With those sweet thoughts, Renuka fell asleep happily in the pale moonlight that filtered through her window.

Issun Bōshi

If you were to search for stories from Japan, the story of Issun Bōshi, or the one-inch boy, surfaces time and again. This fairy tale from Japan is similar to the story of Tom Thumb in English folklore. There are varying twists to the story depending on who does the telling but the essence of the story—of a little boy and his adventures and misadventures—remains the same. It is a story of hope and achievement.

Once upon a time, an old childless couple in Japan wished for a child. They were tired of living alone and went to a shrine and prayed long and hard for a child of their own. They begged the gods and said, 'Please, please let us have a child, no matter how small. We may be old, but we promise to take good care of our child.'

Soon, a son was born to them. But the child was so tiny that it was only as large as the old man's fingertip. The old couple named the tiny child Issun Bōshi because in Japanese, *issun* is a measure of approximately three centimetres and *bōshi* means son.

The old couple were delighted and brought up their son with a lot of love and attention. The years passed happily, and Issun Bōshi learnt many subjects and acquired many skills. But despite growing older with each birthday, he came to the sad realisation that he

would never grow any bigger in size. He decided that despite looking minuscule, he was now an adult and needed to leave home and find his place in the world.

One day, he came to his parents and asked for their permission to venture out to explore cities beyond his home. He said he wanted to be a Samurai warrior like others around him. So, his parents gave him a sewing needle for a sword, a sheath made of straw, a soup bowl for a boat and chopsticks for oars. Bidding his parents goodbye, and with their blessings, Issun Bōshi left home to start his journey.

Soon, Issun Bōshi came to a river. Using his soup bowl boat and chopstick oars, he crossed the river and reached the city. He walked onwards and soon came to the front of a huge mansion. Thinking he could work in this grand house as a servant, Issun Bōshi called out to the guard, saying that he was available to work. Unfortunately, no one heard his call or even noticed his presence. It was then that Issun realised that he was still in the shadow of the guard's feet, so he came out into the clearing. Soon, Issun Bōshi was granted permission to see the lord of the house. Everyone liked the charming and intelligent young man; the lord was most fascinated by the little man and his confident, smart personality. Within days, Issun Bōshi had become the personal attendant of the lord's daughter.

One day, the lord's daughter took Issun Bōshi along with her on a journey to Kiyomizu Temple. On their way, two large, mean ogres blocked their path. Issun Bōshi immediately drew his sword and ran towards the ogres. The ogres laughed. One ogre caught the tiny man and swallowed him whole in one gulp. Fortunately, Issun Bōshi was still alive, and he used his sword to stab the ogre's stomach. The ogre shrieked loudly and was so overcome with pain that he threw up. And with that, Issun Bōshi was free again. Issun Bōshi immediately lashed out with his sword and stabbed the other ogre in his eye. The ogres dropped their magic hammer and ran away, howling.

The lord's daughter recognised the hammer for what it was and told Issun Bōshi that he could ask for anything he wanted, even all the treasures of the world. Issun Bōshi immediately asked the hammer to make him a normal-sized, full-grown man. In a flash, Issun Bōshi transformed into a full-grown, handsome warrior. He then married the lord's daughter and, together with his parents, they lived happily ever after.

KAYAMKULAM KOCHUNNI AND THE MONEYLENDER

Kayamkulam Kochunni lived in the early nineteenth century in Kayamkulam in the Allapuzha district of Kerala. The stories about Kayamkulam Kochunni are part of folklore in Kerala. The man was revered as a folk hero. In fact, there is a shrine erected in his memory near the town of Kozhenchery. The Kochunni narratives immortalised in Malayalam in the Aithihymala are full of adventure and drama, escape from prison and much more. They are based on the life of a man who was sometimes a thief, sometimes a hero. In a way, Kochunni was a Robinhood figure who was a nuisance to law enforcers and reviled by the wealthy for their losses. But, he was also a hero to the downtrodden and poor who benefitted from his generosity.

There was once a rich and miserly man whose chief interest in life was amassing wealth and ensuring that no one had access to his money. This wealthy man lived during the time when Kochunni's deeds were on everyone's mind. People knew that Kochunni was not just a skilled thief, he was also a master of Kalaripayetu—a form of traditional martial arts—which he put to good use during robberies. The rich miser was desperate to ensure his wealth could not get into Kochunni's hands. He built a house with granite stone and fortified it with wooden panels to make it impenetrable. When people asked him 'why both stone and wood?', he would reply, '... to keep Kochunni away!'

The story of this double-panelled house reached Kochunni's ears, and he was determined to find a way to break in and teach the rich man a lesson. But he also knew that he would have to devise a clever plan. He learnt that the rich man had given his neighbour, Krishna Kurup, a loan of 1,000 rupees against the collateral of a few pieces of the neighbour's family jewellery.

One day, the rich man came home with a bag and gave it to his wife. He said that Kurup had paid him back, and he wanted his wife to put the money in the treasure chest. He also wanted her to get him the stored jewellery so he could return them to Kurup, who was waiting by the ghats. It was already getting dark, and he wanted to complete this transaction before nightfall.

A few days later, Krishna Kurup came to the rich man with a bag and said, 'Here is the money I borrowed from you, with interest. I would like to take my jewellery back.' The rich man looked aghast. He called out to his wife. He said to Kurup, 'What is this madness? I have already returned the jewellery, and I have already received the money. How could this have happened?'

The rich man's wife ran to the money chest and pulled out the bag that had supposedly been handed over to her husband. When they looked inside, they

saw that the bag was heavy with metal chips and not gold coins.

That is when the rich man realised that he had been tricked. Before they could weep or wail, they heard a knock at the door. Kayamkulam Kochunni was standing there. He gave the bag of jewels to Krishna Kurup and handed back the money to the rich man. He then said, 'I am not interested in stealing just to steal. I took your money because I wanted to teach you a lesson. It is important for all who have wealth to pay attention to the needs of others who may be less fortunate. Greed is an unhealthy vice.'

Kochunni then told them a story to reinforce his thoughts.

'A long time ago, a rich man lived in a village in Kerala. His house was full of utensils of different shapes and sizes. He had all kinds of utensils that one could expect to find in a house as magnificent as his. Whenever there was a ceremony in the village, the villagers would borrow the rich man's utensils and return them as soon as possible for fear of having to pay double, as was expected.

This system of borrowing utensils for a certain sum of money had been going on for many years. However, one day, after an event, a young man turned up at this rich man's doorstep with more utensils than he had actually borrowed. When the rich man enquired about the extra utensils, the young fellow replied that the utensils had been blessed with children and that he was simply returning the offspring with the parents. The wealthy man rejoiced at such a stroke of luck. A few days later, the young man returned to rent more utensils for his sister's marriage. The rich man, remembering his recent unexpected gains, began to count his additional fortune. A fortnight went by, and there was no news of the young man or the borrowed utensils.

One evening, the rich man saw the young man running towards him, looking anguished. When asked, the young man remorsefully replied that three of the utensils had passed away and the last two had just committed suicide. The rich man was incensed. He realised that he was being tricked. He grabbed the young man by his shoulders and asked him how could inanimate pieces of steel and silver kill themselves? He demanded that all his utensils be returned at once. At this, the young man smiled and reminded the rich man that he had accepted the unexpected gain without question, but he was unwilling to do the same for the loss. He asked, if it made sense for utensils to give birth, why couldn't they die or commit suicide? The rich man realised his folly and, acknowledging his greed, asked the young man to keep the utensils as a reward for having opened his eyes.'

Kammapa the Monster
— and —
No King as God

Kammapa is a mythical creature that shows up in stories from the Sesotho or Sotho tribe of southern Africa. He is described as 'a shapeless, gluttonous monster that swallows everything living. As it gets larger and larger the more it swallows.' Thus, he was a creature of never-ending greed. Many folk tales and fables from Africa describe the origin of humankind, as in the case of Kammapa's story. Kamappa the Monster is a retelling of a story originally shared in the southern Bantu language of the Lesotho area of Africa. The story, No King as God, *in this African collection, is from southwestern Nigeria on the western part of the continent, where Yoruba is the spoken language.*

KAMMAPA THE MONSTER

Once upon a time, in a faraway land, there was a terrible monster named Kammapa. The monster's sport was devouring humans, and soon, he ate all the humans in Africa. In the end, the only person left in the world was an old woman, who, fearing all that she saw around her, had gone into hiding.

Though she was the last woman in the world and alone, the old woman gave birth to a boy who emerged adorned with magical amulets. Ecstatic, she named her son Lituolone, in honour of her god. As with divine births, the boy was a full-grown, strong young man by nightfall.

Lituolone asked his mother why they were alone in the world. 'Where are the other people?' he demanded.

His mother told him about the monster Kammapa and described Kammapa's destruction of the world. Without a moment's hesitation, Lituolone grabbed a knife and went to fight the monster. But unfortunately, before he could use his knife, Kammapa swallowed Lituolone in one gulp.

Since Lituolone was swallowed whole, he found himself unharmed in the beast's stomach. Lituolone used his knife to cut his way out. As he tore apart the beast's belly, thousands of other humans also began to escape. That is how Africa was re-populated, and Lituolone become the founder of the Sesuto tribe.

NO KING AS GOD

It was said that in the beginning, there was only the sky above and water and wet marshland below. God Olorun ruled the sky, and Goddess Olokun ruled below. But this caused a problem. Where would other living creatures that needed dry land live?

God Obatala reflected on this dilemma and came up with a plan. He went to Olorun and asked permission to create dry land for living creatures to inhabit. He was granted permission.

Obatala then sought the advice of Orunmila, the eldest son of Olorun and the god of prophecy. He was told that he would need a gold chain long enough to reach the earth below, a snail's shell filled with sand, a white hen, a black cat, and a palm nut, all of which he was to carry in a bag. Everybody decided to help. The gods contributed what gold they had, and Orunmila supplied the remaining items for the bag.

When everything was assembled, Obatala hung the gold chain down from a corner of the sky, placed the bag over his shoulder and started the downward climb. He used the chain as a rope-like ladder but

when he reached the end of the chain, he saw that he still had some distance to go to reach the ground.

He heard Orunmila's instructions from above. He had to pour the sand from the snail's shell, and at the same time, release the white hen. He did as he was told. He noticed that the hen had landed on the sand and had begun scratching and scattering it about. Wherever the sand and landed, it formed dry land. The bigger piles became mounds of hills and the smaller piles were called valleys. Obatala jumped down to a hill and named the place LIFE. The dry land now extended as far as he could see.

Next, Obatala dug a hole, planted the palm nut, and saw it grow in a flash. The mature palm tree dropped more palm nuts on the ground and each nut grew immediately into a mature tree. The process kept repeating itself, and soon the landscape was dotted with palm trees. Obatala settled down on land with the cat for company.

Many months passed, and Obatala grew bored with his routine and his life. He decided that he would create beings like himself to keep him company. He dug the sand and found soft clay with which he could mould figures like himself. Obatala soon tired of this activity as well and decided to take a break.

Obatala realised that wine could be made from palm trees and quickly set out to make it. He drank bowl after bowl and was soon in a stupor. He then returned to his task of creating beings out of clay but, because he was drunk, he fashioned many imperfect figures. Without realising this, he called out to Olorun to breathe life into his creatures.

The next day, when he awoke, Obatala realised what he had done. He swore never to drink again. He also made a solemn promise to take care of those who were deformed and thus became 'Protector of the Deformed'.

The new people built huts as Obatala had done, and soon, the place became a city. All the other gods were happy with Obatala's work and visited the land often. But Olokun, the ruler of all below the sky, was not happy. She had not been consulted by Obatala and was angry that he had usurped so much of her kingdom.

Once, when Obatala was away from his land and visiting his home in the Sky, Olokun summoned the great waves of her vast oceans and sent them surging across the land. She unleashed wave after wave until much of the land was underwater, and many people had drowned.

Many people fled to the highest land and beseeched the god, Eshu, who had been on a visit to earth. They asked him to return to the sky and report to Orunmila what had happened to them. Eshu demanded the sacrifice of goats before he delivered the message. The people sacrificed some goats, and Eshu returned to the sky.

As soon as Orunmila heard the news, he climbed down the golden chain to the earth and cast spells that caused the flood waters to retreat. And that was the end of the great flood. According to folklore, this is how the vast dry African land reappeared.

Ganesha and the Moon

Of the many gods worshipped by Hindus, Ganesha, Ganapati or Ganapathi, is probably the most popular and perhaps, the most beloved. Many Hindus see him as one of the most important god, and he is loved for being the most child-like and human in terms of his temperament. Ganesha has a special place in the hearts of all people.

An invocation to Ganesha, the remover of obstacles, commences all rituals and important occasions in India, even today. There are many wonderful stories from Ganesha's childhood and adult years about the Elephant God's mischief, wisdom and playfulness. This parable, loved by both laymen and devotees, explains the waxing and waning of the moon.

One day, Ganesha was riding home on his vehicle, the mouse, after having feasted on a large meal of sweet modakas. This traditional sweet of rice dumplings filled with coconut and jaggery was his favourite, and he had eaten to his fill. Suddenly, Ganesha's mouse spied a snake on the ground.

Suddenly Ganesha's mouse spied a snake on the ground. While trying to avoid stepping on it he missed his step and tripped. Ganesha also lost his balance, toppled and fell hard on the floor. In the fall, his large stomach, which was full of modakas, burst open. The sweets tumbled out.

Chandra, the moon, looked on at this spectacle and burst out laughing. Ganesha hurriedly tied his stomach together using the careless snake as a belt. But he was offended by the moon's delight at his discomfort. Ganesha threw his broken tusk at the moon and cursed

that he would never be welcome in the heavens and never shine again.

In those days, the moon shone brightly every night, and this curse of darkness was a problem to all. Without moonlight, young lovers were sad. Poets exclaimed that their verse lost its poetry, and songwriters were silent. Since the moon no longer shone at night, the sun blazed bright throughout the day and mothers exclaimed that their children were refusing to sleep. It was equally sad in the heavens where the moon was absent. The gods acknowledged that something had to be done about Ganesha's curse.

Taking a plate of the choicest foods, the gods approached Ganesha and pleaded with him to reconsider his curse. They did not need to reason with him for long. Kind-hearted Ganesha fully understood that the earth and its inhabitants could be in trouble without the moon's light.

Ganesha remembered an incident from his childhood. When he was very young, he had teased a cat by pulling its tail and pushing and rolling the animal on the floor. The cat had cried out and tried to run away, but Ganesha was too little to realise that he was causing it pain and kept on teasing it. Soon, Ganesha got tired of playing with the cat and went home to his mother. When the child climbed onto his mother's lap, he noticed that she had red marks and some scratches on her face and body and was in discomfort. Ganesha hugged his mother and asked her what had happened. He was worried about her. She smiled and told him that she was the cat and that he had thoughtlessly hurt her. Ganesha immediately understood that all actions have an impact on others.

Ganesha told the gods that he would amend his decision and attempt to withdraw his curse on the moon. He explained that his words had been pronounced more as an impulsive outburst than out of anger. But a curse, once issued by a god, can never be fully withdrawn. He could only soften its blow. Ganesha stated that the moon would never be restored to its full daily brilliance. It would shine again, but its light would grow in increments. The moon would start as a sliver and become a full moon only once every twenty-nine-and-a-half days. Therefore, there would only be two full moons in a month. Ganesha also said that people should never look at the moon on the fourth day of the festive fortnight as scandal would befall them, and they could become a laughing stock as he had been. This superstition persists even today, and many people still avert their eyes from the moon on Ganesh Chaturthi.

TENALI RAMAN AND THE RED PEACOCK

Tenali Ramakrishna, or Tenali Raman, was a court poet in the kingdom of Krishnadevaraya of the Vijayanagara empire. He was born in a village in Andhra Pradesh in the early sixteenth century. The written history about him describes a man of uncommon talent and wisdom. This story reveals Tenali's legendary cleverness, strategic skills and sharp wit. Tenali tales are popular, especially in South India, as folktales that teach about intelligent action. These stories are popular bedtime stories for children.

King Krishnadevaraya was a good and just king, but he was too trusting of his courtiers, including those who were greedy and criminal-minded. This naivete bothered his wisest courtier, Tenali Raman. Krishnadevaraya's other weakness was that he liked opulence and grandeur and was often guilty of spending too much from his treasury to ensure the majesty of his palace. Many ministers exploited the king's fascination with the 'unusual' and took advantage of his wealth and generosity. In fact, there was one devious minister who had built a large fortune over the years by selling trinkets (that he claimed were treasures) to the king.

One day the same minister brought a red peacock to the court and pronounced that it was an exotic bird procured from a faraway place with great difficulty.

The king was captivated by the red feathers and the unusual quality of the peacock. Since it had such a distinct plumage, he was interested in purchasing it for the palace gardens. The king asked the minister what the peacock was worth. The shrewd minister, noticing the king's interest, cheerfully announced that the bird was worth a hundred gold coins.

Tenali Raman, who was in the court and had watched the bird's arrival, immediately stood up and stated that the king should wait to make a payment for such an exotic bird. He said, he, Tenali Raman, would travel to the faraway place and ensure that the bird could survive outside its natural habitat.

The king heard Tenali Raman and immediately knew he had made a plan worth supporting. He agreed that he would only purchase the exotic peacock after Tenali Raman had returned from his travels.

Tenali Raman went home, but instead of going on a long journey, he made enquiries in the town to discover the truth behind the devious minister's find. As expected, Tenali realised that the exotic red peacock

was not as unusual as it was made out to be. He learnt that the greedy minister had bought a brown peahen and asked a painter to paint its feathers a bright red colour. Tenali assured the frightened painter that no harm would come to him for divulging the minister's secret, and then enlisted the painter and his artistic talents for a new plan.

Tenali returned to court a few days later and said he had a gift of ten red peacocks for the king. The king was delighted and offered to pay Tenali Raman 1,000 gold coins. Tenali Raman stopped him and said, 'Your Majesty, that amount is not the actual cost of these birds.' The king looked puzzled. Tenali spoke again, 'I would like to be paid with a bag of red powder, a bucket of water, and one gold coin to reward the skill and labour of the artist who helped me.' Tenali Raman then pointed to the painter he had brought to court.

The king realised that he had been tricked by the greedy minister. He immediately prepared to exile the scoundrel, but Tenali Raman stopped the king from banishing the minister. Instead, Tenali reminded the king of his own role in this story. Tenali Raman

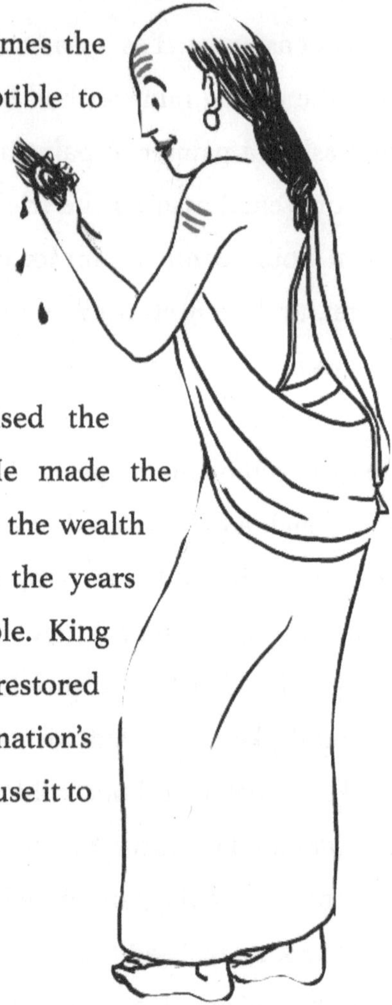

recounted the many times the king had been susceptible to various unnecessary expenses because of his flamboyant interest in the exotic and unusual.

The king recognised the error of his ways. He made the greedy minister return the wealth he had amassed over the years by hoodwinking people. King Krishnadevaraya then restored the gold to the nation's treasury and vowed to use it to serve the people better.

THE LION AND THE DONKEY

Historians believe that the stories that comprise the Panchatantra *were probably composed in the Sanskrit language in 300 CE. The book,* Panchatantra, *is divided into pancha (five) tantras (systems or chapters) that describe the science of wise conduct.*

Patrick Olivelle, professor of Sanskrit at the University of Austin, Texas, US of A, stated in his book Pañcatantra: The Book of India's Folk Wisdom *that more than 200 versions of each Panchatantra story are available in as many as fifty languages. Numerous retellings and revisions of the original stories from the* Panchatantra *are available in the public sphere. Clearly, these tales with their life lessons have been popular for a very long time.*

This story is a retelling from one of the chapters of the Panchatantra. *Although the original composition of this story has not survived, it has been translated into English several times. I have retold the tale keeping the moral intact as that is the essence of the original narrative structure. The language used in this retelling is modern, while the style, cadence and dialogue have been formulated in a classical form. Though donkeys are known to be herbivorous, this story is written as it was found and presents the animal differently.*

Did you know that the Panchatantra *was originally written as a manual for a king to learn how to rule wisely?*

Once upon a time, in a big forest, there lived a lion. He was both powerful and vicious in his pursuit of his prey. He was also a very skilled hunter. Whenever he was hungry, he would go in search of food, and within minutes he would catch an animal to satisfy his appetite.

But, as the years went by, the lion became old and his limbs became feeble. He did not have the strength or the speed to catch prey as easily as he did earlier. His eyesight also became weak, and he could not spot the food he needed to hunt and eat. He realised that he would soon die unless he came up with a clever plan.

One day, the lion was sitting in the forest when he heard the loud sound of a braying donkey. Instantly, the lion came up with an idea. He looked around for it and found the animal grazing not too far away.

The lion approached the donkey carefully as he didn't want to scare him. Speaking in a gentle tone, the lion said, 'Dear friend, I heard you bray. You make the loudest sound of all the animals in the forest. I think we can work together. Will you be my partner?'

The donkey was surprised. He could not believe that the ferocious lion was asking a donkey to be his partner. But, he was flattered by the offer. Without hesitation, he agreed.

The lion elaborated on his plan. 'This is my plan,' the lion explained. 'When we notice a group of animals gathered in the forest, I will go and hide. You should then make the loudest sound that you can. The animals will be startled and perhaps even scared by your braying. They will run here and there, and many will most likely run towards where I am hiding. I am sure that as soon as an animal or two are within reach, I will be able to catch at least one of them. You can have a share of my catch after I have had a meal.' (A non-vegetarian donkey is unheard of, but perhaps this donkey had unique superpowers for braying and eating!)

The donkey was honoured and proud to be the lion's assistant. He did exactly as he was told. Whenever he saw animals gathered in a group or a herd, he brayed in the loudest voice he could muster. The sound surprised and scared the animals, just as the lion had predicted. They dispersed randomly, and a few ran towards the lion hiding in the bushes. The lion immediately pounced on one of the unfortunate animals and killed it for his meal. In this manner, both the lion and the donkey kept themselves fed and nourished for a while.

Unfortunately, the arrogant donkey soon began to think too much of himself. He began to feel at par with the lion and felt like one among the strongest animals in the forest. He was certain that by now all the animals were afraid of him. He began strolling throughout the jungle, braying loudly and scaring other animals. The donkey became so haughty that he soon forgot about the security his partner, the lion, had provided him all this while.

One day, as the donkey was wandering in the forest to scare the animals, a leopard heard him braying. The leopard immediately recognised the sound of a donkey. He wasn't frightened by its volume. He ran towards the sound, pounced on the foolish donkey, who was away from the protection of his partner, and tore him apart. The donkey became a satisfying meal for the leopard.

The lion later came upon the carcass and thought sadly, 'False pride always proves to be harmful.'

How the Animals Got Sunlight

This popular Native American story is also a lesson in perseverance and effort in times of difficulty. It recognises the value of inventive thinking. The story's moral is familiar, and the lesson it communicates resembles those found in Indian classics like the Panchatantra *and the Jataka tales. As we see in this story, Native American folk tales also anthropomorphise, or attribute human characteristics to animals and other beings, to provide teachable narratives.*

This story provides a springboard to further discover the importance of sunlight in our lives. We can learn that the energy from the sun is transferred from plants to animals when animals graze and eat plants. We also understand that animals benefit from the sun's effect on their bodies as sunlight on the skin produces vitamin D, which is vital for forming strong bones.

A long time ago, all animals lived in a part of the world that was very dark. Though they had spent many days in such a shadowy existence, they had never really accepted it. They moaned that they could not see each other. They cried that they could not see the food they ate. They lamented at not being able to enjoy the beauty of the place around them. They could distinguish the fragrance of plants and flowers and the smell of their surroundings in the dark. That was all. The animals were not a happy group. They stumbled and bumped into each other, sometimes falling and scraping themselves. Eventually, they decided to take charge of their unfortunate situation.

'Let's call a meeting and make a plan,' the wise Owl said. He was wise not only because he was old, but also because he was one of the animals who could see better than many others in the dark. 'What we need is light,' Owl said.

'Light! Light!' the animals exclaimed. 'That sounds wonderful. But, from where will we get this light?' they cried in a chorus.

'I hear there is light on the other side of the world,' Owl said. 'But it will be a long and dangerous journey to get there. Whoever chooses to go may not find their way, and if they do, they may never be able to return with the light. It is a dangerous mission and not for everyone!'

The animals shook their heads sadly and moped in defeat. Who would volunteer to undertake this difficult journey, they wondered. They shuddered in the dark.

Suddenly, Possum spoke up. 'I will make the journey. I have a furry body and bushy tail. When I reach this light, I will take some of it, wrap it in the fur of my tail and carry it back here.'

The animals were excited by this plan. They thanked Possum for his offer and sent him off on the journey with cheers and salutes.

Possum began walking east towards the light. It took him a long time, but after many days, he thought that he could see some light. As he got closer to the sun, the light was so bright that he had to half close his eyes to move forward. That is why, even today, the eyes of possums look like slits.

Finally, Possum was close enough to grab a small ball of light from the sun. He wrapped it carefully in the fur of his tail and began the long walk back. Sadly, the sun's light was so hot that Possum got lost and took even longer to return. By the time he returned to the animals, the hot sunlight had burnt all the fluffy fur off his tail. He had also dropped and lost the ball of light. This is why, even today, a possum's tail has no hair.

The animals were disappointed that they would have to remain in darkness. They wailed and shouted out in frustration. Just then, a voice spoke up. It was Vulture. 'I will go,' Vulture said. 'It looks like we need a volunteer with wings who can make the journey more swiftly and return just as quickly.' Vulture thought about the trip and made his plan. 'Possum dropped the light by transporting it on his body. I will carry it on my head and bring the light back to the animals.'

Vulture spread his wings and took off into the sky towards the east. Soon, he saw the light of the sun in the distance. Excited, he flew quickly towards it and grabbed a ball of light. Balancing it on his head, he began to fly back. But the ball of light was just as hot as Possum had found it, and the blazing sunshine and heat of the sun made Vulture feel dizzy. He flapped in the wrong direction, and the sun burnt all the feathers off his crown. This is why, even today, vultures have bald heads. The piece of sun that Vulture was transporting fell to the ground, and he returned home unsuccessful in his quest.

The animals realised that they would have to continue living in the dark. They were all very sad. Just then, a soft voice spoke up. The animals could not see who the voice belonged to, but it was Old Lady Spider. She said, 'Let us try one more time. I may be old and small, but I think I can bring you the light you want.'

Old Lady Spider thought long and hard. She realised that it was important that she did not get lost. She understood that the light was bright and may be

hot to touch, so she planned well. First, she found some clay. Using her eight hands, she made a small pot to transport the light. Then, she wove a web around the pot and attached it to her back so that it was secure. She began her journey by weaving a web that would guide her return. She set out, travelling east and spun her thread behind her. When she reached the sun, she quickly pinched off a bit and put it in the clay pot. Then, she followed her thread home.

When Old Lady Spider returned with a bit of the sun, the animals had light and saw clearly for the first time. They looked at old Lady Spider with gratitude and noticed in the light that she was old and frail. Yet, she had persisted and succeeded when others had failed. Old Lady Spider was applauded. From then on, people learnt to make pots with clay that could be dried in the sun. And from then on, just like Old Lady Spider, spiders weave their webs in the cool early morning as they don't enjoy the blazing heat of the sun's light!

THE MOUSE AND THE MERCHANT

This story is from the Jataka tales, which were written between 300 BCE and 400 CE. The tales pertain to Gautama Buddha and his previous births, both in human and animal form. The merchant, the hero of this story, shows how innovation in business is often more important than the capital used to grow the business. The Jataka tales impart valuable virtues that can be learnt.

A long time ago in Benaras, the king's advisor was on his way to the palace when he saw a dead mouse lying on the road. He said to those who were walking with him, 'Even this dead mouse has its use, and if a man sets his mind to improving his life, he can always do it.'

A passer-by heard these words and picked up the mouse. As he was walking with the dead mouse in his hand, a man walking by called out to him and said, 'May I buy this dead mouse from you? I will give you two copper coins. My cat is going to be very happy with this mouse.'

The man was pleased to get the coins in return for the dead mouse. He used the coins to buy a few slices of sweet cakes and bottles of water. He then stood at the side of the road with the sweet cakes and water in his hand.

Very soon, a few flower-pickers walking by after a day's hard work stopped by the side of the road to drink water. They asked the man if they could have the sweet cakes to eat in exchange for a bunch of the flowers that they had picked that day. The man was happy to make this transaction, and the flower-pickers were pleased with their refreshments.

In the evening, the man sold the flowers in the city. With some of the money he earned, the man bought more sweet cakes and returned the next day to sell them to the flower pickers. The man continued to carry out this trade daily, and soon, he was making a tidy profit.

One day, there was a big storm with heavy rains and high winds. While the man was walking around in the city, he noticed that the palace gardens were a mess with many branches broken off from trees in the bad weather. He saw the king's gardener trying to tidy the garden and offered to help if he could keep the branches that he helped gather. The tired gardener, grateful for the assistance, agreed to the deal.

The man called a few children playing across the street and asked for their help. The children were glad

to collect all the branches for just one sweet cake each. The man now had accumulated plenty of firewood. Soon, the king's potter, who was walking by, saw the large bundle of branches that the man was carrying and offered a large sum of money for the wood. The potter needed firewood for his kiln. The man sold the wood to the potter and, in return, was paid handsomely. The potter was generous enough to give the man a few pots as well.

With the money he made from the sale of firewood and the pots, the man (who could now be called a merchant) opened up a shop to sell refreshments. One day, a man who sold grass and hay stopped at the shop to buy sweet cakes. The merchant generously offered the man refreshments at no cost. He was very grateful and asked the merchant how he could pay him back for his generosity. The merchant smiled and said, 'One day, I will ask you.'

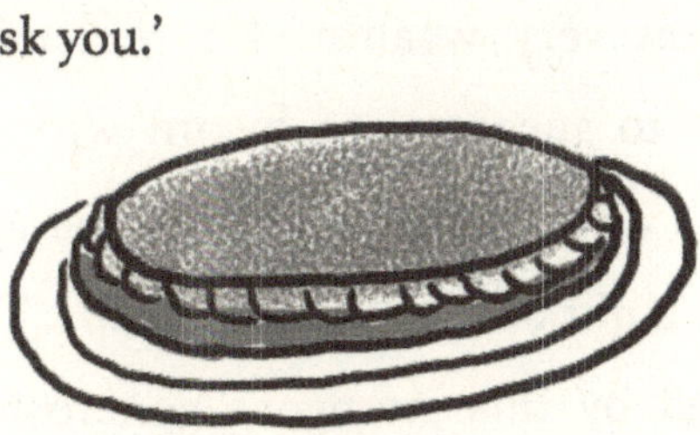

A week later, the merchant heard that a horse dealer was coming to the city to sell 500 horses. The merchant remembered the man who sold grass and hay and his promise. He soon acquired the grass at a low cost and sold it to the horse dealer for a tidy profit.

The following week, a foreign ship came to the port. The merchant had a beautiful ruby and gold ring made with his earnings and offered it to the ship's captain as a gift. The captain was delighted with this unexpected gift and remarked that he had never seen anything so lovely. Soon enough, the merchant and the captain became good friends. The merchant told the ship's captain that he would direct all the ship's crew to appropriate shopkeepers at the port so they could buy what they wanted. In exchange for customers, each shopkeeper gave the merchant a commission.

In a few years, the job of a middleman had made the merchant very wealthy. He remembered that his journey to success had begun with the words of the king's advisor, so he went to the advisor and offered him a gift of 1,00,000 gold coins. The advisor was shocked by this stranger's generosity, but the merchant showed his gratitude and told him the story of his success and fortune.

The advisor thought, 'It would not be good to lose the talents of such an energetic man. I will give him my daughter's hand in marriage.' The marriage took place in grand style. Many years later, after the wise advisor died, the king recognised the value of the advisor's son-in-law and appointed the man to the high position of court advisor. And people said to themselves, 'With energy and ability, great wealth comes even from small beginnings.'

Aesop's Fables

It is not exactly known when the first book of Aesop's Fables *was written, since the stories were originally handed down orally from one generation to the next. However, historians believed that Aesop lived from about 620 to 560 BCE and was most likely the creator of these short stories. Each of these stories illustrates a particular moral and together Aesop's Fables teach various lessons to children. They were cleverly told and presented human problems through the dilemmas of animal characters. A moral fable with animals as characters is called an apologue. Debate remains over whether the Greeks learnt these fables from Indian storytellers or if it was the other way around, or if the influences were mutual. These selected retellings are a few of the most well known of Aesop's stories.*

THE ANT AND THE GRASSHOPPER

BELLING THE CAT

THE DOG AND THE SHADOW

THE CROW AND THE PITCHER

THE ANT AND THE GRASSHOPPER

One bright summer day, an ant was on his way to his burrow with corn on his back, when he saw a grasshopper singing cheerfully and playing in the sun. The grasshopper called out to the ant and said, 'What are you doing, my friend? Why are you working on such a lovely day? Come and play with me.' The ant replied that he was preparing for winter by storing the food that would not be as readily available in the colder months.

'Why bother about winter now?' said the grasshopper. 'We have plenty to eat now, and we can worry about winter after we are done playing.' The grasshopper continued to play while the ant toiled away.

Soon, it was winter, and the grasshopper noticed that food was not easy to come by. On the other hand, the ant seemed to be living off what he had stored in

the summer. The grasshopper realised that he had been careless and unthinking about his future. He learnt that it is always best to prepare for the days of necessity.

BELLING THE CAT

Once a group of mice got together to talk about the harassment they faced from the mean cat in their neighbourhood. They decided that they had to come up with a plan to outwit their common enemy.

'Things are getting really difficult for us,' said one old mouse. 'This treacherous cat approaches us when we least expect it.'

'I have a plan,' said a young mouse.

'The problem is that we are always caught unawares. If we could hear the cat as it approaches us, we will all be able to get out of harm's way. I propose we put a bell around the cat's neck so we can hear it ring when he comes close to us.'

Everyone applauded the idea, but the old mouse spoke again, 'That's all very well, and your idea is a good one, but who will volunteer to bell the cat?'

The mice looked at each other and remained quiet. The old mouse wisely said, 'Ideas come easy, but executing them is much harder.'

THE DOG AND THE SHADOW

One day, a dog was walking home with a piece of meat in his mouth. He was looking forward to eating it slowly and peacefully at home. As he walked towards his home, he came to a river. He saw a log that he could use to cross. He stepped onto it and walked forward when he noticed another dog with a piece of meat in its mouth, staring at him from the water. The dog did not realise that he was looking at his own shadow. He was greedy and thought that he would steal the piece of meat from the other dog as well.

He opened his mouth to snap at the other dog and frighten him into submission. Splash! The piece of meat fell out of his mouth into the water. The sad dog realised that he had lost his dinner. With his tail between his legs, the dog went home thinking, 'Beware, you lose the substance by chasing shadows. If you covet all, you may lose all.'

THE CROW AND THE PITCHER

One hot summer day, a thirsty crow was flying in search of water. She looked everywhere, but she could find none. From up above, she noticed a pitcher under a tree and saw the glint of water at its base. The crow tried to put her beak into the narrow spout of the pitcher to drink the water, but the opening was too narrow. The crow was very thirsty, so she thought long and hard and devised a plan.

She dropped pebbles into the pitcher and noticed the water level rising. With each stone she dropped into the pitcher, the water began to rise towards the mouth of the pitcher until it finally reached the opening. The crow could finally dip her beak and drink to her heart's content.

She flew away happy, knowing 'when in a pinch, a good use of one's mind will help'. She learnt, 'Where there's a will, there's a way!'

The Doll in a Red Sari

This is a narrative of hope, initiative and generosity. The story expands our assumptions about the lives of the poor on the urban streets of India. Despite the young boy Ramu's seemingly 'impoverished' state, he is 'affluent' in his cheerfulness, resourcefulness and positive thinking. Despite lack of wealth, Ramu is generous and giving. The story emphasises earning money through hard work, not just for one's own pleasure but to share with others. Ramu's beautiful gift to his sibling is a story of purpose and affection that will inspire and resonate with young readers.

Hai Ram! It is so hot today! This season of loo, the unbearably hot and gusty wind, is the most difficult, especially when one has to stand on the pavement and wait for the traffic light to turn red.

The tar is melting under my feet, and I feel like sitting under the shade of that neem tree. But no, I must persist. It will be so special to buy that beautiful doll, so new and lovely in the shiny red sari, for my sister's birthday.

Gunjan will be so excited. It's really a prize of a doll—with the bright bindi glinting on her forehead, shimmering bangles and the sparkling jewelled slippers on her feet. I must sell six more cloth dusters soon. If I sell a few more, I'll have enough money. That clever doll-maker with her nimble fingers has said it will be mine soon.

I am so pleased that I was able to give her one rupee yesterday instead of fifty paise. She's told me that it will be mine for another two rupees. That doll is so special. I know that Gunjan has been dreaming of a doll for a while now.

Yay! There's a Maruti car! I like Maruti cars. It's so much easier to get my hand in through the window since the car is small and the windows are low. Otherwise, I have to bounce up and down to be seen, and then, I could drop my dusters.

Arre! I must stop this daydreaming. That quick-footed fellow Arun has already reached the car.

Like the saanp in the basket, I'm going to make sure to weave my head back and forth and keep my eyes fastened on the road for a potential customer. I can feel it—today will be my lucky day!

The cars have stopped again. Let me dodge quickly between them. But this time, I must be careful not to trip on a rickshaw's handlebars. Else, the dusters will touch the grimy metal and become dirty. Who will buy them then?

And when the winds start blowing, there will be a

different kind of problem on the roads. All that dust will get in my eyes and stick to the cloth.

'Memsaab, you buy dusters for car? Very good dusters, Memsaab. They clean so well. Eight rupees a dozen! Clean car well, Memsaab. You buy?'

Oh no! The traffic light is green again! I only have a few hours. I can feel it. Rain is coming, and when it does, it will pour and reduce the flow of vehicles on the street.

But I do like the rain. It washes the dust off my body. I love the feel of the falling water that cools me from this heat; and that fresh smell of the earth ... and the trees during the monsoons are really nice.

Yesterday, I played in the puddles and danced and twirled like a peacock in the rain. But today, I'm not going to splash and spray water from the hydrant on the other kids. Fun can wait. I'm on a mission! Today is for Gunjan. I hope it doesn't rain again soon.

Here's a new car with children! It's good when the car has children in it. They don't start rolling up the window as soon as they see me running across the road to them.

And they also say, 'Buy some dusters, Ma!' or 'Look Ma, he's so young and eager!' And they stare kindly at my sweaty face. Of course, I can run after them, but some drivers speed up so soon that it becomes dangerous chasing cars in the traffic.

Oh, there I go, day dreaming again ... and the traffic light has changed!

I better move near the bhutta-wallah on the other side of the road. There definitely seems to be more action on that side. Maybe he'll give me a cob of corn? Yum. He says that the thin bhuttas that are already drying out at the ends and without too many kernels are not really worth selling. The memsaabs haggle with him too much to lower the price.

I'd better hurry to that side of the street or he'll throw that corn to the cows. Or to that stray dog that's always poking around. I hope he'll let me use his lemon wedge to layer the spicy masala. Corn is so delicious with the salt and chilli powder! My mouth is watering already.

Hey! Why are all the cars slowing down? These car horns make such a deafening sound. People can be so impatient. I think that traffic light is acting up again. Great! A traffic jam! This is my chance to be a clever salesman!

'Saab! Good dusters for sale! Big dusters! Wipe car well, Saab! Buy now. Good price! Memsaab will be happy, Saab!'

He won't even look at me. I can't believe people can be so wooden and stern. It doesn't matter. Here's a woman driver. Women are easier. They find it hard to ignore a child.

'Memsaab! Dusters. Good cloth dusters! Eight rupees a dozen. For you, six rupees, Memsaab. Buy dusters, Memsaab?'

No change? Now that is an excuse I am familiar with.

***

The cloud-burst was swift and sudden. The sky darkened, the leaves and debris on the street blew against Ramu's feet, and the rain poured down.

The scene changed dramatically. Cars began to roll up their windows. Ramu poised his feet to run alongside the vehicles if they began to move. The bhutta-wallah put out his choolah, gathered his basket of corn, and began looking for refuge.

The ironing woman folded her table under the mango tree and hastily wrapped the clothes she had been ironing into the folds of a large bedsheet. The other children abandoned their chores and, kicking their heels with glee, danced in the forming puddles.

***

Oh good! The traffic light is still red. This is my lucky day, and I have no more competition. I can almost feel the soft folds of the red sari on Gunjan's new doll. Here's a car with children! No, no, please don't roll up the window!

My shirt is really clinging to me. I hope the notes in my pocket don't get wet.

'Memsaab! Buy dusters please. Large, soft dusters! Clean car well, Memsaab! I'll give three dusters for five rupees.

'Okay Memsaab, for you, four dusters. These are the best dusters, Memsaab—top quality, export quality, Memsaab. Buy now, Memsaab! Four dusters for five rupees. Alright Memsaab, you don't have change? Take five dusters for five rupees—for you, best buy, Memsaab. Thank you, Memsaab. May your kitchen pots always be full, Memsaab.'

Hurrah! I've done it! I've made my sale. There's money for mother and the two rupees for the doll-maker!

I can't wait to see my sister's happy face on her birthday. She will be so happy to have this doll with its red sari. Gunjan, I can't wait to show you what I have for you.

Oh, I love this rain! 'Hey guys! I sold my dusters! I sold ALL my dusters!'

The Story of a Poor Man

The global pandemic has given us more time to reflect. We have seen economic loss, climate crises, and cracks in behaviours and systems. Yet, in a year of tremendous upheaval, change and impermanence, we have witnessed remarkable resilience, kindness and a depth of community care that should not be taken for granted. This story is the memory of a troubling recollection from childhood. The feeling of privilege and guilt affect many, but the story's purpose is to recognise the compassion and hope that is within all of us.

He was thin and bony. His dark eyes seemed to gaze vacantly at the cars and buses that plied the busy Kolkata (then Calcutta) streets, not taking in much. He remained in a huddled position with his skinny knees crossed under him. He was always there on that street corner, like a bundle of tattered rags lying on a sack of coarse cloth.

I saw him every day as I looked out of the window of my car on the way to school. A small bowl lay in front of him.

All this I recall in retrospect. A Wordsworth-ian memory; an 'emotion recollected in tranquillity,' perhaps. The image has sharpened. The weak feeling of sadness that used to surface each time I passed his forlorn figure, with my nose pressed against the car window, my eyes poring through the spotted mist that spread on the glass as I looked, has altered. I felt sorrow

for a brief moment in those days. But then, just as easily, I fell back on the seat to pursue that day's girlish dream. Today, though, the memory has yielded a different feeling, and for some reason, I feel compelled to share this story.

My world is 'great, wide, beautiful, wonderful'—all these glorious adjectives make perfect poetry about life. His life probably had endless monotony. My days include three square meals while he probably had the gnawing ache of an empty stomach. Ours was an existence of polarity, or living lives that are poles apart, and inequality.

I was eleven the day it happened. It was my birthday. The date is clearly etched on my mind. I had stirred out of bed excitedly at 7 a.m. though I had woken up at least half an hour earlier. Being too excited to sleep any longer, I lay quietly in bed. My eyes pretended to be closed while I waited for birthday wishes from those who would come to wake me. My mind raced through all the possible gifts I would receive. I knew there would be books from my sister—a new Enid Blyton mystery, perhaps. Chocolates from my brother, just for his 'little chubs' he would say. And new clothes from Mum and Dad.

They were just outside—I could hear them whispering. My sister giggled; there was the rustle of paper, the sound of Mummy's sari swishing as they all tiptoed to the bed and yelled 'Happy birthday, darling!' After kisses and endearments, it was time to look at the cards. More squeals of delight, followed by the tearing open of gift wrappings and a POLAROID CAMERA! I hadn't even asked for one, but Daddy knew I would love it and could take it on our school's nature study trips.

We could have looked at gifts all day, but it was time for school. Mummy had already bought the tin of sweets I would distribute in class, so going to school was even more special! I wore new socks with my school uniform. Our birthday traditions included wearing something new, but the new outfit could only be worn in the evening at the party.

I was so excited that I could hardly swallow breakfast. I was already hungry for the number 11 shaped strawberry-flavoured cake with pink marzipan roses that had been ordered from Flury's on Park

Street. Marzipan roses were my favourite confection—yum. My tongue could already savour the rich, nutty sweetness of the flowers and their thick green leaves fashioned with almond paste. I had much to look forward to.

My brother allowed me to sit in the front seat of the car, a prized position.

I was eager to get to school, partly because I wanted the school day to end soon so I could have my party and because the teachers would be especially pleasant to me, the birthday girl. Life was wonderful!

The driver slowed at the end of Bhowanipore Road. There was a small gathering of people near that corner of the pavement. Other cars were slowing down and some people were getting off. But I wanted to push ahead, oblivious of the reality.

We passed the crowd with little difficulty. I made it to school, and the day was as perfect as I had hoped. When we returned home at the end of the day, my mother had small bags of coins and little containers of 'birthday food' ready. As the birthday girl, I was to take these offerings and distribute them among the poor people who begged in our neighbourhood. I knew we couldn't feed all the hungry people on the street, but I also knew there was at least one hungry man I could give the food.

Only as we neared the pavement corner did I remember the cars and the crowd that we had sped past in the morning. I began to feel a tinge of apprehension. Where was he? Where was the bent figure who always sat staring vacantly from the same pavement corner? The dusty corner was unoccupied. He had to be there. The realisation of death, an end, the discontinuity of something I had always taken for granted, took a while to touch my eleven-year-old mind. I felt the weight of the food containers and the coins clutched tightly in my fist. I felt disappointed.

The party was a huge success. Everyone I had invited had come. The games were fun, and there were so many gifts in splendid wrappings waiting to be opened. Only, for some reason, I wasn't as happy anymore. The day had soured quite unexpectedly, and I wasn't sure why. A large piece of strawberry-flavoured cake with two pink roses sat pretty on the table. Strangely enough, despite the other dishes being emptied with remarkable speed, the slice of cake with its delectable marzipan roses, cut especially for the birthday girl, remained uneaten all evening.

THE LOVABLE THIEF

This is a story with a twist. Similar narratives have been part of many cultures and their storytelling traditions. I first wrote this as a tale of naughty rabbits in the tradition of the American writer, Beatrix Potter. It was published when I was a teenager in the Hindu's *weekend youth supplement. This version of the story celebrates family, American holiday traditions, and the close connection between a parent and a child. It is an adventure story that showcases filial love and devotion.*

Amma hummed as she worked in the kitchen. Thanksgiving was one of her favourite holidays. Appa had already put the turkey in the oven and made his special corn casserole. Meanwhile, the vegetarian lasagna and eggplant parmigiana were in the warmer for Kiran and Sonali's grandparents, Ammamma and Thatha, who were vegetarian and would be coming soon. It was such a lovely sunny day for the end of November. What a blessing!

Amma had just put the final touches on the family favourite—her special pumpkin pies. She knew that the sweet pies with their soft filling reminded Ammamma of the sugary neyyapams she used to eat as a child in Kerala, in India. Thatha was especially fond of pumpkin pie, so Amma had prepared three pies instead of the usual two. Kiran and Sonali also loved to dip their fingers in the sweet, creamy centre. It was unlikely that there would be any leftover pies that evening!

This Thanksgiving was extra special because Ammamma and Thatha were coming from India for a long vacation. The girls hung around Amma, excited and impatient. Everyone loved the smells of the delicious pies, the steaming broccoli and corn casseroles, and the juicy turkey baking in the oven. Appa had gone out to pick up Ammamma and Thatha from the airport. He promised to bring home a colourful bouquet to dress up the dining table for the occasion. The feasting would begin when they got home!

Amma set the three pumpkin pies out on the window ledge to cool and went to her room to freshen up before dinner. Just then the doorbell rang. Sonali and Kiran could be heard squabbling. The two argued loudly about who would open the door, serve the pumpkin pie, sit next to Ammamma in the car on the next family outing, and everything else they could possibly argue about.

Amma didn't notice that even as the two seemed to be arguing, Kiran quietly opened the backdoor to the garden and sneaked outside. At the same time, the

jangle of keys at the front door announced Ammamma and Thatha's arrival.

As Amma came to the door to greet everyone, she saw only two pies cooling on the window ledge. She rushed to the window and caught a glimpse of a figure running away, holding something in hand. Amma was certain it was one of her special pumpkin cream pies that had been been stolen.'

'Stop, thief!' she shouted, helplessly. Waving her hands agitatedly out of the window, she yelled, 'Come back with my pie, you greedy robber!'

Everyone gathered around to see what the excitement was about. Appa looked around and noticed that Kiran was nowhere to be seen. 'Where's Kiran?' Now, it was not just one missing pie; there was one missing child too!

Ammamma hugged Sonali to comfort her. The five-year-old's face looked like it was about to burst into tears. Nobody noticed that Sonali was hiding a mischievous smile as she buried her head into the folds of Ammamma's sari. Everything was chaotic and noisy, with everyone talking all at once. Thatha and Appa went outside to look for the thief, but they were back in a

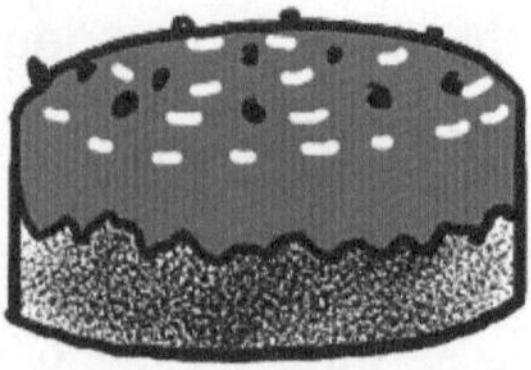

few minutes without success. Meanwhile, tummies were rumbling, so the unhappy group slowly made their way to the dining room.

The sound of a doorbell broke the silence. And it rang and rang. It was loud and incessant. Clearly, someone was impatient. Thatha got up to answer the door. Everyone followed.

At the front door was Kiran, proudly holding a delicious pumpkin pie in her hands. 'Surprise! Surprise!' she sang, smiling broadly. Before they could even say, 'Where have you been?' and 'Where did you find the pie?' the whole story came spilling out.

The children had planned the entire 'robbery'. Kiran was supposed to be the thief, and the reason for the robbery was that they wanted to decorate the pie with a special message in chocolate frosting. The message read: THANK YOU AMMA and APPA. WE LOVE YOU.

What a wonderful surprise it was! Ammamma

and Thatha beamed at the resourcefulness of their grandchildren. Appa, who was ready to scold Kiran, just smiled, and Amma didn't know what to do or say anymore. She could hardly believe that the girls had been so clever with their secret. She took the pie in her hands and laughed as she hugged her daughters.

They soon learnt that Kiran had arranged for her friend's mother, who lived across the street, to do the lettering on the pie with a homemade chocolate frosting. Sonali played her part in the game by pretending to worry about Kiran's disappearance. Everything had been planned carefully so they could say a special 'thank you' to Amma and Appa on Thanksgiving.

The now cheerful family sat down to dinner. After all that excitement, they were ravenous and looked forward to the Thanksgiving Day feast that awaited them. There was very little conversation between mouthfuls of delicious food. Everyone was lost in happy thoughts. It would be a very long time before they forgot the story of the lovable thief and her affectionate assistant.

Lockdown Stories

The 100-word format of these 'Lockdown Stories' forces the writer to question each word and use the most appropriate word or phrasing to advance the story. It supports Flaubert's 'mot juste' (the right word) and is a fun and challenging exercise.

The themes are all connected to being indoors and the quiet of lockdown. The stories reinforce that sometimes we only have our imagination for company, especially during a pandemic! I enjoyed this creative exercise and encourage readers to try their hand at it as well.

Inheriting a sweet shop

A story from the perspective of a pet

An autumnal walk

I discovered a secret miniature world in my bedroom

Seeing a ghost

Accidentally bringing home a witch's cat

A holiday on Mars

An animal that came back from extinction

INHERITING A SWEET SHOP

We are sheltering at home, limiting our movements and trying to maintain a physical distance from our family and friends. It is a difficult time for so many. The streets are deserted, shops are shuttered and seats everywhere are empty. But I have inherited a sweet shop, and I plan to make the most of my inheritance! Since my pantry is full of sugar and flour, syrup and honey, dried fruits and nuts, I'm stirring, mixing, baking, eating and sharing. It fills the heart to see the smiling faces of surprised neighbours who found yummy sweet treats outside their homes.

A STORY FROM THE PERSPECTIVE OF A PET

I am not sure why this happened, but both Mum and Dad are 'working from home' these days. I'm not sure if they are working or are on a holiday, but they are here, indoors, and they don't ever leave other than for walks. It started out as fun. I mean, who doesn't like being patted and cuddled? But they won't leave me alone. At all! What happened to REST? Whenever they step out of the house, it's 'for exercise' and guess who's their favourite companion? I'll be honest, my aching legs are ready for them to return to work.

AN AUTUMNAL WALK

Empty sidewalks. An eerie quiet. Only an occasional car passes by on the road. I'm on a walk during quarantine, and it's a different experience than it used to be. It's not that there is no noise, but that the quiet is broken by cheeps of birds, not the blare of horns or the squeal of tyres. I hear the drip of water from a faucet through an open window. I pass and almost hear the whoosh of the wind as it teases my hair. My footsteps sound loud on the pavement. And soft, if I choose a gentler gait.

I DISCOVERED A SECRET MINIATURE WORLD IN MY BEDROOM

I have discovered a secret miniature world in my bedroom. And in it, my imaginary friends, my imaginary food and my imagined stories, are part of everything I once knew outside of here. It's as though I have another world in this place where I am in charge. Where I can make up my own rules. And where I can do exactly as I please. The freedom for fun is tremendous. But there's just one problem. I hear my parents calling me for dinner. It seems I will have to leave this world for the other one for a while.

SEEING A GHOST

My brother was a great storyteller. I liked when he made us laugh, but sometimes his stories were not funny. My sister and I clung together after spooky tales, but she could fall asleep. My imagination, always triumphed. That night, every shadow looked like a ghost. I quaked under the bedsheets until, finally, sleep came. Suddenly, I felt a form near the bed and a touch on my shoulder. My eyes shot open. I saw a ghost. I screamed, turning on the light! I saw white pyjamas. A breeze from the open window had blown them over to the bed!

ACCIDENTALLY BRINGING HOME A WITCH'S CAT

She rubbed against my legs and meowed in the sweetest tone. I was bowled over. I always loved cats; burying my face in their soft fur and cuddling their warm body close, so I could hear the hum of their purr in my ear. So, of course, I picked her up and brought her home. But this animal surely was no ordinary cat! She was a magical creature like the cat in the story 'Puss in Boots' and my life changed from then on. I mean, who wouldn't like owning a witch's cat that cooks, cleans and makes the bed!

AN ANIMAL THAT CAME BACK FROM EXTINCTION

Wouldn't it be perfect if dinosaurs came back to earth today? They could be the army that we need—to blow away, trample on, scorch with fire, or swallow up with giant teeth—the virus that has spread from place to place and country to country so swiftly. Dinosaurs are so large, fierce and magnificent that they will form an impenetrable wall of resistance. The virus wouldn't have a chance to enter, forget about it taking over the world! The dinosaur is the perfect animal to come back from extinction, and it could be the perfect weapon that destroys COVID-19!

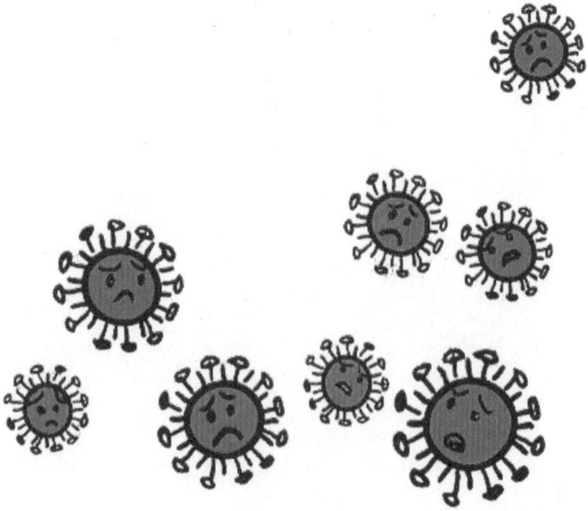

A HOLIDAY ON MARS

Cancelled sports events and graduations. Empty shelves in grocery stores. Money lying with airlines for missed flights when reschedules went awry. Parents buying art supplies and books for their children and cocktail recipes and drinks for themselves. New subscriptions to streaming platforms and investments in better cameras and mics for Zoom. Expectant mothers worried about how they will give birth safely. Florists, massage and physical therapists scrambling to reinvent themselves while restaurateurs turn creative to avoid shutting doors. Places of worship going online. Bills unpaid, clothes unworn. Feeling claustrophobic. We are all so ready even for a holiday on Mars!

ANOTHER BOOK BY

SHOBHA THAROOR SRINIVASAN

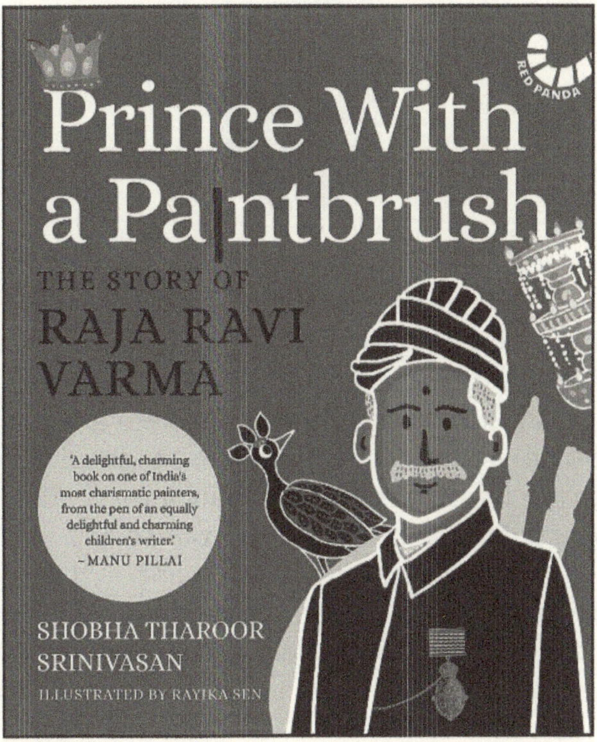

The red panda is a reddish-brown mammal with a long, ringed tail and a raccoon-like face. This endangered animal is found in the forests of eastern Himalayas and is the state animal of Sikkim. Also called firefox, the cat-sized animal is largely herbivores but also eats insects. The red panda uses its bushy tail to balance and wrap it around its body to stay warm in the chilly mountains. A victim of deforestation, there are less than 10,000 animals remaining in the wild.